'Possums and the EMPTY TOMB

PICTURE BOOK APOLOGETICS *with* JAMES & RUTH

by J.D. CAMORLINGA

Picture Book Apologetics, Whittier 2014

Printed in the United States of America

First Printing, 2014

All scripture quotations, unless otherwise indicated, are taken from the Holy Bible, New International Version®, NIV®. Copyright ©1973, 1978, 1984, 2011 by Biblica, Inc.™ Used by permission of Zondervan. All rights reserved worldwide. www.zondervan.com The "NIV" and "New International Version" are trademarks registered in the United States Patent and Trademark Office by Biblica, Inc.™

ISBN: 978-0692300664

Picture Book Apologetics
Whittier, CA

www.PictureBookApologetics.com

ACKNOWLEDGEMENTS

We give all glory to the Father who created us, to the Son who redeemed us and to the Spirit who sealed us; Praise be to Him!

DEDICATION

For brother Jordan, who helped set us on this journey, and for inquisitive young minds everywhere. May you see the truth of God which is declared by the stars themselves, and may you live your lives accordingly, boldly declaring His name, confident that what you believe is true.

James and Ruth love to talk about Jesus' resurrection.

Some days they read the story, some days they ask their parents big questions, and some days they are amazed that He died for their sins.

One evening, while they were playing in a thicket,
James and Ruth found a big, hollowed out rock.

"Hey Ruth," James said. "Do you think
Jesus' tomb looked like this big rock?"

Just as Ruth began to answer, three small 'possums peeked out of the rock.

"Who are you?" asked the biggest 'possum.

"What are you doing by our rock?" asked the medium 'possum.

"And who is Jesus?" asked the smallest 'possum.

James and Ruth took turns answering the 'possums' questions. They told them that Jesus died on a cross and was buried and that He rose again three days later. The 'possums weren't convinced.

"What if the disciples just stole Jesus' body and hid it so that people would **think** He came back to life?" asked the biggest 'possum.

"Disciples and friends of Jesus were killed for telling people that He came back to life. They wouldn't have been willing to die if they **knew** it was just a lie. That would be silly," said James.

"Not only that," Ruth said, "but there were many soldiers guarding Jesus' tomb. A few sad disciples couldn't have sneaked past that many guards without being seen. Plus, if the guards **had** noticed them, the disciples wouldn't have stood a chance."

"Those soldiers were really tough. Fighting them would be like a single person fighting a tank!"

"Sometimes I get turned around in the forest at bed time and sleep in the wrong thicket!" said the medium 'possum. "Maybe Jesus' friends just got lost, went to the wrong tomb, and only **thought** it was empty!"

"If that happened, wouldn't the people that killed Jesus tell everyone where the right tomb was?" Ruth asked. "Jesus was buried in a tomb that belonged to a man named Joseph. It wasn't a secret. When people started saying 'Hey! Jesus is alive,' the Jews and Romans could have easily proved them wrong, but they didn't, because they couldn't, because the tomb was really empty."

The littlest 'possum flopped on the ground.
"What if He was just playing 'possum?" she asked. "Maybe He
pretended He was dead and then pretended He came back to life!"

"That's a good guess," James answered, "but you see, Jesus was hurt very, very badly the day He was put on the cross. He was hurt so badly that everyone that saw Him and touched Him said He was dead; even the people that were trained to know better! If He was that hurt, there is no way he could have rolled away the HUGE tombstone and then fought off the guards."

"And He sure couldn't have fooled 500 people into thinking
He came back to life in a perfect body!" Ruth added.

"Jesus wasn't the kind of person who would tell a whopper like that," James said.

The three little 'possums whispered to each other
for a long time. Then they nodded their heads.

"It sounds like Jesus really did come back to life!"
the 'possums squeaked. They were convinced!

So, as the sun slowly set behind the hills, James and Ruth smiled from ear to ear, said goodbye to the little 'possums, and scampered home.

"If you declare with your mouth, 'Jesus is Lord,' and believe in your heart that God raised him from the dead, you will be saved."

Romans 10:9

Practical Exercise

Park your car in a safe place with the emergency brake engaged. Ask your children to push the car. Here are some discussion points to consider:

- The average car weighs about 4000 pounds; that is 2 tons! It is estimated that the average round grave stone, like the one used for Jesus' tomb, weighed about 3500-4000 pounds and was rolled into a slanted groove to block the tomb's entrance.

- Not only would Jesus' disciples have needed to roll the 2 ton stone up the incline, they would have needed to do so without being detected by the many well-trained soldiers stationed at the tomb.

- Does it seem likely that a severely wounded man, such as Jesus, could have pushed the stone aside?

The Resurrection as Evidential Apologetics

- The resurrection is proof - evidence - of Christianity's truth. The empty tomb stands as a testament to that truth. No other religion's veracity depends upon a historical event.

- Jesus could have exited the tomb without rolling away the stone, but He didn't. He wanted it to be obvious that He had risen. He then made sure that people knew He was alive (Acts 1:1-3)! Early Christians did not have to take the resurrection on faith; they witnessed the empty tomb (John 20:11-13), they clung to him (John 20:17), and they touched the holes in his hands and side (John 20:27). They had ample evidence of Jesus' resurrection.

Find suggested reading and more resources written by experts in their fields, at
www.YouthApologeticsNetwork.com

Adults,

The Christian faith is a historical faith, meaning it is rooted in history, but there are some people that attempt to undermine the historicity of the Bible. One of their primary fixations is the resurrection of Jesus Christ. Why is the resurrection important to them (and to us, for that matter)? Paul explains that if Jesus was not raised from the dead our faith is useless, and we should be pitied above all men (1 Cor. 15:14-19). If Jesus was not raised, He would still be dead and would still be paying for our sins. If He is still paying for our sins, we are unforgiven and unsaved, because the payment has not been made in full. Furthermore, our faith would be a farce. However, if He *was* raised from the dead, the payment for our sins *is* complete, and we need only repent and believe in Him to be saved! Our faith truly hinges on the historical resurrection of Jesus Christ.

Our hope is that this book will help you guide your child through a simple refutation of often repeated arguments against the resurrection, while also equipping them to respond with courage and kindness when their beliefs are challenged. We pray that this book will inspire deep conversations between you and your child about our resurrected Savior, and will encourage them to love Him in ever-deepening ways.

In Christ,
J.D. Camorlinga

DR. GARY HABERMAS' MINIMAL FACTS APPROACH

The following facts are widely agreed upon, boast strong evidence and are best explained by Jesus' historical resurrection.

1. Jesus died by crucifixion.
2. He was buried.
3. His death caused the disciples to despair and lose hope.
4. The tomb was empty.
5. The disciples believed they experienced literal appearances of the risen Jesus.
6. The disciples were transformed from doubters to bold proclaimers.
7. They preached the message of Jesus' resurrection in Jerusalem.
8. The resurrection was the central message.
9. The Church began and grew.
10. Orthodox Jews who believed in Jesus made Sunday their primary day of worship.
11. James (a family skeptic) was converted to the faith when he saw the resurrected Jesus.
12. Paul (a skeptic and persecutor of early Christians) was converted to the faith.

For more apologetics materials about the resurrection, visit GaryHabermas.com

Also available from Picture Book Apologetics:

Pig and the Accidental Oink
(The Kalām cosmological argument)

Chameleon's Can of Worms
(Defense against relativism)

Coming Soon:

The problem of evil